Pebble® Plus

Animal Groups

A Herd of Elephants

by Amy Kortuem

Raintree is an imprint of Capstone Global Library Limited, a company incorporated in England and Wales having its registered office at 264 Banbury Road, Oxford, OX2 7DY – Registered company number: 6695582

www.raintree.co.uk
myorders@raintree.co.uk

Edited by Abby Colich
Designed by Tracy McCabe
Original illustrations © Capstone Global Library Limited 2020
Picture research by Eric Gohl
Production by Kathy McColley
Originated by Capstone Global Library Ltd
Printed and bound in India

978 1 4747 8526 6 (hardback)
978 1 4747 8532 7 (paperback)

British Library Cataloguing in Publication Data
A full catalogue record for this book is available from the British Library.

Acknowledgements
We would like to thank the following for permission to reproduce photographs: iStockphoto: amrishwad, 17, Cheryl Ramalho, 19; Shutterstock: BlueOrange Studio, 9, Christopher Robin Smith Photography, background, Inspired by Africa, 15, Johan Swanepoel, cover, 1, Ninejaru, back cover (top), 5, Paul Hampton, 7, Roger de la Harpe, 11, Villiers Steyn, 13, Yuda Chen, back cover (bottom), 21

Contents

What is a herd?

The ground shakes. Loud sounds
fill the air. What is all this noise?
It is a group of elephants!
Elephants live in Africa and Asia.
Most elephants live in herds.

Groups of elephants are called herds. Eight to a hundred elephants live in a herd. The herd lives and finds food in one area. This is its territory.

All females live in a herd.
Their young live with them.
The oldest and largest female
leads the herd. Some males live
alone. Others live in small groups.

Eating and eating!

Herds walk through their territory. They look for food. Elephants eat only plants. They eat leaves, fruit, bark and grass. They use their tusks to dig for roots.

tusks

Elephants grab food with their long trunks. The trunks reach tall branches and grab food from the ground. Trunks suck up water too.

trunk

Elephant calves grow

Female elephants give birth
to calves.

Calves drink milk from their
mothers. After a few months,
the calves can eat grass.

The herd keeps calves safe from danger. The lead female opens out her ears. She looks bigger. She charges! Predators run away. The herd is safe.

Calves grow into adults. Females stay with the herd. Males leave when they are around 13 years old. They look for mates in other herds. They may fight with other males for mates.

Elephant talk

Elephants make many sounds. They make a rumbling noise to find each other. Scared calves squeal for help. When elephants are surprised or charging, they trumpet loudly.

Glossary

calf young elephant

charge rush at in order to attack

mate one of a pair of animals that join together to produce young

predator animal that hunts other animals for food

rumble deep, heavy, continuous sound

squeal sharp, high sound

territory land on which an animal grazes or hunts for food and cares for its young

trumpet loud, shrill cry of an animal, especially an elephant

Find out more

Books

Amazing Elephants (Walk on the Wild Side),
Charlotte Guillain (Raintree, 2014)

Elephants, James Maclaine (Usborne, 2011)

Elephant vs Rhinoceros (Animal Rivals), Isabel Thomas
(Raintree, 2017)

Websites

www.bbc.co.uk/bitesize/clips/z87w2hv
Watch this video comparing elephants to humans.

www.dkfindout.com/uk/animals-and-nature/elephants
Find out more about elephants.

Comprehension questions

1. How does the herd protect young elephants?
2. What sounds do elephants make? What do they mean?
3. Why do you think it is better for an elephant to live with a herd than alone?

Index